Assessment Book

PEARSON
Scott
Foresman

Editorial Offices: Glenview, Illinois • Parsippany, New Jersey • New York, New York
Sales Offices: Parsippany, New Jersey • Duluth, Georgia • Glenview, Illinois •
Coppell, Texas • Ontario, California • Mesa, Arizona

www.sfsocialstudies.com

Program Authors

Dr. Candy Dawson Boyd
Professor, School of Education
Director of Reading Programs
St. Mary's College
Moraga, California

Dr. Geneva Gay
Professor of Education
University of Washington
Seattle, Washington

Rita Geiger
Director of Social Studies and
    Foreign Languages
Norman Public Schools
Norman, Oklahoma

Dr. James B. Kracht
Associate Dean for
    Undergraduate Programs
    and Teacher Education
College of Education
Texas A&M University
College Station, Texas

Dr. Valerie Ooka Pang
Professor of Teacher Education
San Diego State University
San Diego, California

Dr. C. Frederick Risinger
Director, Professional
    Development and Social
    Studies Education
Indiana University
Bloomington, Indiana

Sara Miranda Sanchez
Elementary and Early
    Childhood Curriculum
    Coordinator
Albuquerque Public Schools
Albuquerque, New Mexico

Contributing Authors

Dr. Carol Berkin
Professor of History
Baruch College and the
    Graduate Center
The City University of New York
New York, New York

Lee A. Chase
Staff Development Specialist
Chesterfield County
    Public Schools
Chesterfield County, Virginia

Dr. Jim Cummins
Professor of Curriculum
Ontario Institute for Studies
    in Education
University of Toronto
Toronto, Canada

Dr. Allen D. Glenn
Professor and Dean Emeritus
Curriculum and Instruction
College of Education
University of Washington
Seattle, Washington

Dr. Carole L. Hahn
Professor, Educational Studies
Emory University
Atlanta, Georgia

Dr. M. Gail Hickey
Professor of Education
Indiana University-Purdue
    University
Fort Wayne, Indiana

Dr. Bonnie Meszaros
Associate Director
Center for Economic Education
    and Entrepreneurship
University of Delaware
Newark, Delaware

ISBN 0-328-08192-2

4 5 6 7 8 9 10-V016-12 11 10 09 08 07 06 05

© Scott Foresman 1

Contents

To the Teacher

One way to evaluate the success of your social studies instruction lies in using the assessment options provided in **Scott Foresman** *Social Studies*. These options will help you measure students' progress toward social studies instructional goals.

The assessment tools provided with **Scott Foresman** *Social Studies* can

- help you determine which students need more help and where classroom instruction needs to be reinforced, reviewed, or expanded.
- help you evaluate how well students comprehend, communicate, and apply what they have learned.

Scott Foresman *Social Studies* provides a comprehensive assessment package as shown below.

Assessment Options Available in Scott Foresman *Social Studies*

Formal Assessments	✓ What did you learn? PE/TE ✓ Unit Review, PE/TE ✓ Unit Tests, Assessment Book ✓ Test Talk Practice Book
Informal Assessments	✓ Teacher's Edition Questions ✓ Close and Assess, TE ✓ Try it! PE/TE ✓ Think and Share, PE/TE ✓ Courage in Action, PE/TE ✓ Hands-on History, PE/TE
Portfolio Assessments	✓ Portfolio Assessment, TE ✓ Leveled Practice, TE ✓ Workbook Pages ✓ Unit Review, PE/TE ✓ Curriculum Connection, TE
Performance Assessments	✓ Hands-on Unit Project, PE/TE ✓ Internet Activity, PE ✓ Unit Review: Think and Share, PE/TE ✓ Scoring Guides, TE

Overview of Assessment Book

Unit Tests

The Unit Tests are a tool to evaluate students' understanding of social studies concepts and their ability to apply and analyze the concepts. There is a four-page, reproducible test for each unit in the Student Book.

Students are asked to fill in blanks, complete sentences, choose a correct answer from a series of possible responses, draw an answer, match items, and read/complete a map, chart, or graph.

Some of the questions carry the same Test Prep symbol as found in the Student Book. The icon tells students that a particular question is formatted the same way it would appear on a standardized test.

At the back of the Assessment Book, there is an answer key for each Unit Test.

Part 1: Content Test
The two-page content test includes a series of multiple choice questions covering levels of thinking from knowledge to comprehension, application, and analysis.

Part 2: Skills Test
The two-page skills test checks students' knowledge of and ability to apply the social studies skills taught in the Student Book.

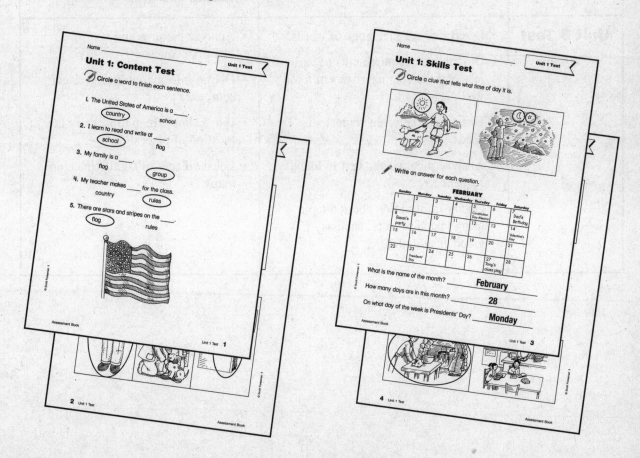

Unit Tests: Objectives Assessed

	Content Objectives	Skills Objectives
Unit 1 Test	• Determine the meanings of words. • Understand that people belong to many different groups. • Identify the responsibilities of authority figures in the school and home.	• Obtain information about a topic using pictures. • Read and create a calendar. • Understand that people belong to many different groups. • Give examples of rules. • Compare past and present.
Unit 2 Test	• Determine the meanings of words. • Give examples of how people in a neighborhood depend on each other. • Explain similarities and differences between life in cities, towns, and on farms.	• Identify and describe the human characteristics of places, such as types of houses. • Construct a map using basic map symbols. • Locate places using the four cardinal directions.
Unit 3 Test	• Determine the meanings of words. • Describe the requirements of various jobs and the characteristics of a job well-performed. • Distinguish between wants and needs. • Analyze pictures and text to identify sequence. • Obtain information about a topic using visual sources, such as graphics and pictures.	• Analyze pictures and text to identify sequence. • Obtain information using visual sources. • Use a simple map to identify the location of places. • Locate places of significance on maps.

	Content Objectives	**Skills Objectives**
Unit 4 Test	• Determine the meanings of words. • Identify ways that natural resources can be used and reused.	• Identify main ideas from print sources. • Distinguish among past, present, and future. • Create a time line. • Identify physical features such as landforms and bodies of water. • Distinguish between land and water on globes and maps.
Unit 5 Test	• Determine the meanings of words. • Identify contributions of historical figures who have influenced the nation. • Obtain information about a topic from visual sources such as pictures.	• Use cardinal directions on a map. • Obtain information about a topic from visual sources such as diagrams.
Unit 6 Test	• Determine the meanings of words. • Obtain information about a topic from visual sources such as pictures. • Identify the role of markets in the exchange of goods and services. • Describe how household tools and appliances have changed. • Describe how technology has changed communication. • Describe how technology has changed transportation.	• Recognize words that help make a prediction. • Create visual and written material, including graphs. • Use a decision-making process to identify a situation that requires a decision.

NOTES

Unit 1: Content Test

 Circle a word to finish each sentence.

1. The United States of America is a _____.

country   school

2. I learn to read and write at _____.

school   flag

3. My family is a _____.

flag   group

4. My teacher makes _____ for the class.

country   rules

5. There are stars and stripes on the _____.

flag   rules

Draw pictures of two groups you belong to.

 Circle people who help you follow school rules.

Unit 1: Skills Test

 Circle a clue that tells what time of day it is.

 Write an answer for each question.

FEBRUARY

Sunday	Monday	Tuesday	Wednesday	Thursday	Friday	Saturday
1	2	3	4	5 Constitution Day–Mexico	6	7 Dad's Birthday
8 Susan's party	9	10	11	12	13	14 Valentine's Day
15	16 Presidents' Day	17	18	19	20	21
22	23	24	25	26	27 Tony's class play	28

What is the name of the month? _____

How many days are in this month? _____

On what day of the week is Presidents' Day? _____

Circle the picture that shows a group.

 Draw a line under a good rule for school.

Brush your teeth.

Raise your hand to talk.

Turn off the TV.

 Circle the picture that shows the past.

© Scott Foresman 1

Unit 2: Content Test

 Circle a word to finish each sentence.

1. North America is a _____.

   law   continent

2. Many neighborhoods make up my _____.

   community   ocean

3. A mayor is one kind of _____.

   state   leader

4. Atlantic is the name of a big _____.

   law   ocean

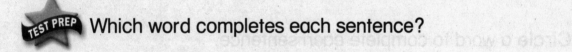 **Which word completes each sentence?**

1. Littering is against the _____.

   a. leader   b. law

   c. ocean   d. state

2. Florida is a _____.

   a. leader   b. lake

   c. continent   d. state

Draw one person who helps in your neighborhood.

Draw a leader in your community. **Drawings will vary.**

```
┌──────────────────────────┬──────────────────────────┐
│                          │                          │
│                          │                          │
│                          │                          │
│                          │                          │
│                          │                          │
│                          │                          │
│                          │                          │
│                          │                          │
│                          │                          │
└──────────────────────────┴──────────────────────────┘
```

 Circle a word to complete each sentence.

I. A town community is not as big as a ____.

      city   farm

2. Going to a parade on July 4th is a ____.

      law   custom

3. The United States is part of ____.

      Florida   North America

Unit 2: Skills Test

 Color the two houses that are alike.

Color the school red.

Color the park green.

Color the lake blue.

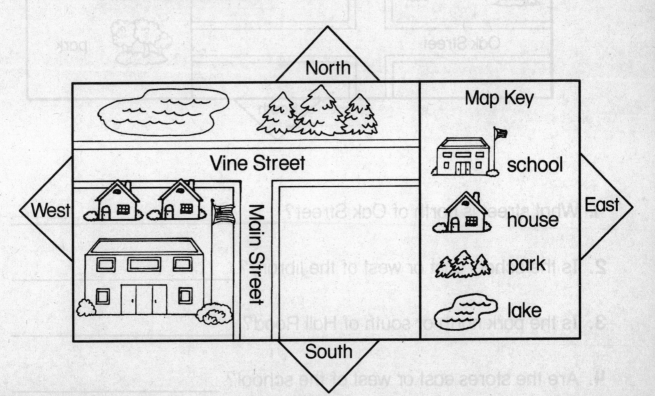

North

Vine Street

Main Street

West

East

South

Map Key

school

house

park

lake

Name _____

 Look at the map.

 Write an answer for each question.

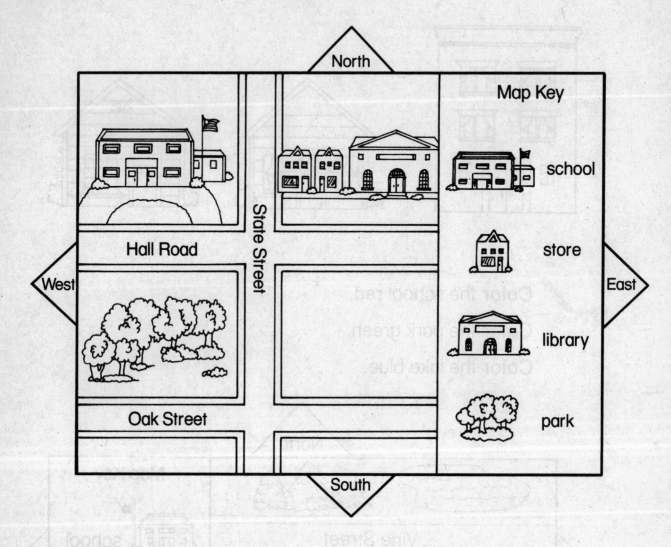

1. What street is north of Oak Street? _____

2. Is the school east or west of the library? _____

3. Is the park north or south of Hall Road? _____

4. Are the stores east or west of the school? _____

© Scott Foresman 1

Unit 3: Content Test

 Circle a word to finish each sentence.

1. Food, water, and clothing are ____.

   needs   jobs   volunteers

2. Toys, games, and TV are ____.

   needs   tools   wants

3. Hammers and nails are a builder's ____.

   tools   service   transportation

4. Cars, trucks, and vans are kinds of ____.

   needs   jobs   transportation

 Which word completes each sentence?

1. A person who works for free is a ____.

   a. job   **b.** volunteer

   c. service   **d.** transportation

2. Things that are grown or made are ____.

   a. goods   **b.** wants

   c. needs   **d.** tools

Draw someone making or growing goods.

Draw someone doing a service job.

Goods	Services

 Draw a line under the answer to each question.

1. Which is a need?   toys   food

2. What is your job at school?   to learn   to eat

3. What can you do with money?   cook it   save it

4. Who grows the food we eat?   farmers   teachers

5. Which is a kind of transportation?   a house   a truck

© Scott Foresman 1

Unit 3: Skills Test

 Write *first*, *next*, and *last* to show the order.

_____   _____   _____

 Write names of people at home.

Jobs at Home

Jobs	Helpers
Set the table.	
Make the beds.	
Cook dinner.	

Name _____

Trace Lee's route on the map.

 Write words to complete the sentences.

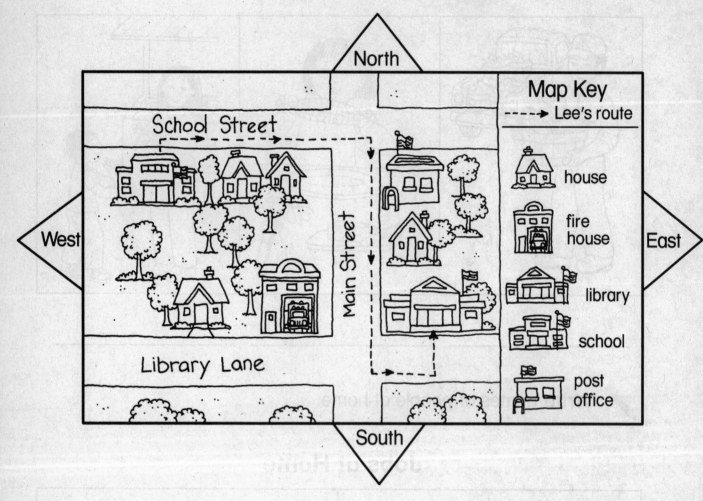

1. Lee starts at the _____ .

2. Lee goes _____ on School Street.

3. Lee goes _____ on Main Street.

4. Lee goes _____ on Library Lane.

© Scott Foresman 1

Unit 4: Content Test

 Circle a word to finish each sentence.

I. A hill is not so high as a ____.

    lake   mountain

2. An ocean is much bigger than a ____.

    natural resource   lake

3. Air, water, and soil are examples of ____.

    endangered   natural resources

4. The water in a ____ usually moves toward a lake or the ocean.

    lake   river

 Which word completes the sentence?

I. For days now, the ____ has been rainy.

    a. weather   **b.** natural resource

    c. history   **d.** river

2. That book tells the ____ of our state.

    a. mountain   **b.** history

    c. plain   **d.** lake

Write how you use each natural resource.

air _____

water _____

soil _____

is _____

 Draw how you can help save a natural resource.

Draw a line under the answer to each question.

1. Which is a large body of salt water?   pond   ocean   hill

2. Which do we get from trees?   oil   corn   paper

3. Who were the first farmers in Iowa?   Seneca   Ioway   Shoshone

4. What can you recycle at school?   cans   water   paint

Unit 4: Skills Test

 Look at the picture and read the story.

Jim wants to save trees. He doesn't take paper he doesn't need. When he writes, he writes on both sides. He uses the recycling bin to throw paper away. That way, the paper can be made into something for Jim to use again.

 Draw a line under the main idea of the story.

Jim hikes in the woods.

Jim wants to save trees.

Jim is a good writer.

 Draw to show what you did each day.

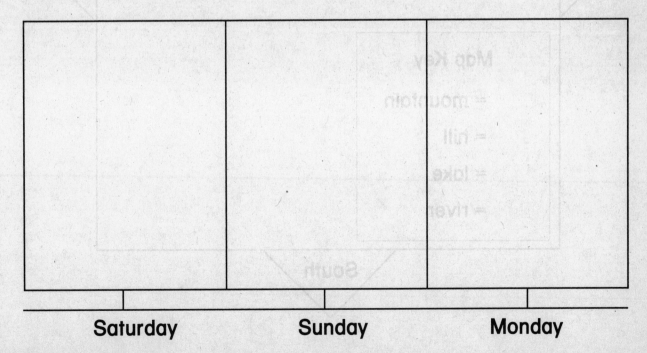

| Saturday | Sunday | Monday |

Draw symbols on the map key.

Then use the key to make a map.

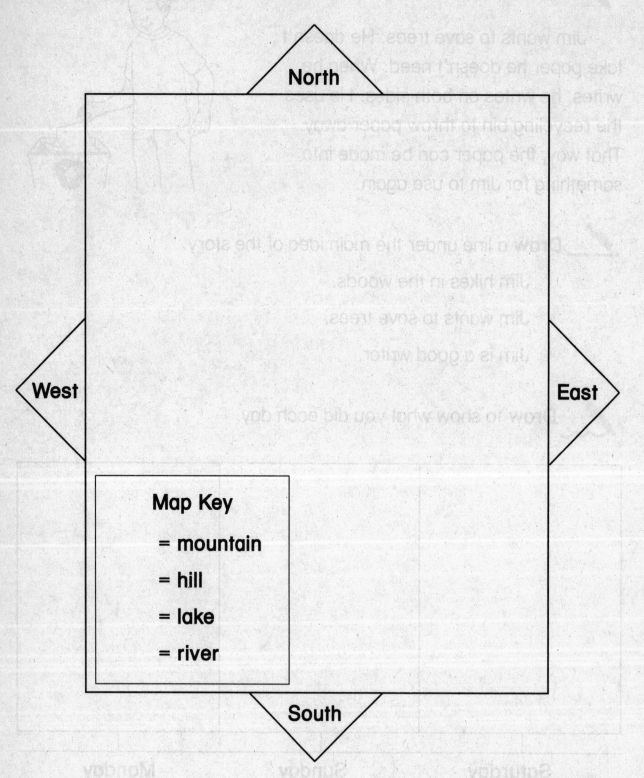

North

West

East

Map Key

= mountain

= hill

= lake

= river

South

Unit 5: Content Test

 Circle a word to finish each sentence.

1. Atlanta is the _____ of the state of Georgia.

   capital   colony   vote

2. To vote, a _____ of the United States must be 18 years old.

   holiday   colony   citizen

3. Presidents' Day is a _____ in February.

   freedom   holiday   colony

4. A person's right to make choices is called _____.

   freedom   capital   holiday

 Which word completes the sentence?

1. Virginia was once a _____ of England.

   a. vote   **b.** colony

   c. holiday   **d.** capital

2. George Washington was our first _____.

   a. citizen   **b.** capital

   c. holiday   **d.** President

© Scott Foresman 1

Write a letter to match each picture with a sentence.

a. The first people in North America were Native Americans.

b. Columbus landed on an island near North America in 1492.

c. The Pilgrims came to North America on the *Mayflower*.

d. Women who lived in the colonies made their own candles.

e. George Washington was a famous leader during a war with England.

f. We have holidays to honor people from the past.

 Write to complete this sentence.

I am a citizen of the state of _____

and the country of _____ .

Unit 5: Skills Test

 Draw three pictures to retell this story.

That first winter was very hard for the Pilgrims. The Wampanoag helped the Pilgrims. They showed Pilgrims what crops to plant. The Pilgrims hunted and fished for other food. Later, they celebrated with the Wampanoag.

I	2	3

 Circle the correct words.

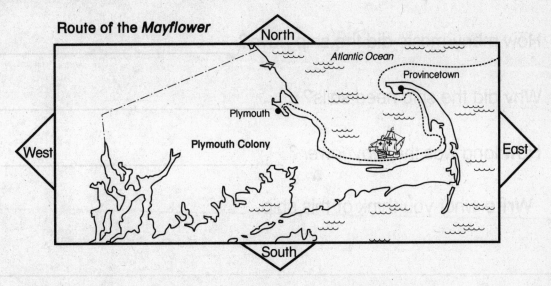

Route of the *Mayflower*

North

Atlantic Ocean

Provincetown

Plymouth

West

Plymouth Colony

East

South

The Pilgrims sailed across the (Atlantic, Pacific) Ocean.

They landed first at (Boston, Provincetown).

They finally settled at (Plymouth, Boston).

Answer the questions about the diagram.

Mayflower

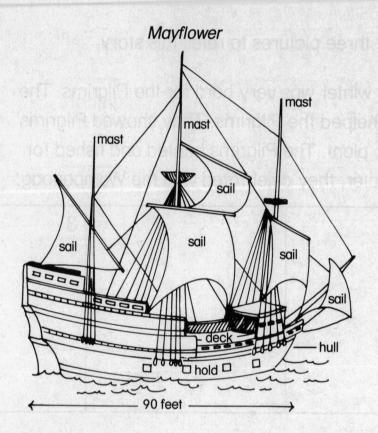

I. What does the diagram show? _____

2. How many masts did the ship have? _____

3. Why did the ship need sails? _____

4. How long was the *Mayflower*? _____

Write what you think of this ship.

_____

_____

_____

Unit 6: Content Test

 Write a word from the box to finish each sentence.

market	communicate
world	invention

1. Earth is the name of our _____.

2. The printing press was a great _____.

3. Talking is one way to _____.

4. Goods are bought and sold at a _____.

 Which word completes the sentence?

1. People who invent things are _____.

   a. worlds   **b.** markets

   c. inventors   **d.** inventions

2. People use telephones to _____.

   a. invention   **b.** world

   c. communicate   **d.** inventor

Look at each picture and read the question.

 Circle the letter of your answer.

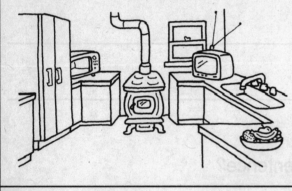

1. What do people do here?

    a.   buy things they need

    b.   make decorations

    c.   borrow books to read

2. What looks very old?

    a.   the sink

    b.   the TV set

    c.   the stove

3. Who invented this?

    a.   Thomas Edison

    b.   Alexander Bell

    c.   Mae Jemison

 Write to complete these sentences.

Long ago, people traveled by _____.

Today, people travel by _____.

© Scott Foresman 1

Unit 6: Skills Test

 Write to predict.

Luis has a pen pal. The pen pal lives in Japan. Luis and his pen pal write to each other often. They tell each other about their families and friends.

One day, Luis got a new pet. He was so excited! He drew a picture of his dog. He put himself in the picture too.

What will Luis do?

_____

Use the bar graph to answer the questions.

Best Pets

	1	2	3	4	5
Dogs					
Cats					
Fish					
Birds					

How many children like dogs? _____

How many children like fish? _____

What pet do the children like best? _____

Nan's family wants to buy a pet. Dad wants a dog. Mom wants a cat. Her brother wants a hamster. Nan wants a goldfish. The family has to decide which pet to buy.

Where can Nan look to gather information about each type of pet?

 Circle 3 things that would help Nan gather information about pets.

An encyclopedia

A dictionary

The Internet

A newspaper

A book about pets

An atlas

Top-left panel

Name _____

Unit 1: Content Test

Circle a word to finish each sentence.

I. The United States of America is a ____.
(country)   school

2. I learn to read and write at ____.
(school)   flag

3. My family is a ____.
flag   (group)

4. My teacher makes ____ for the class.
country   (rules)

5. There are stars and stripes on the ____.
(flag)   rules

Top-right panel

Name _____

Draw pictures of two groups you belong to.

Drawings will vary.

Circle people who help you follow school rules.

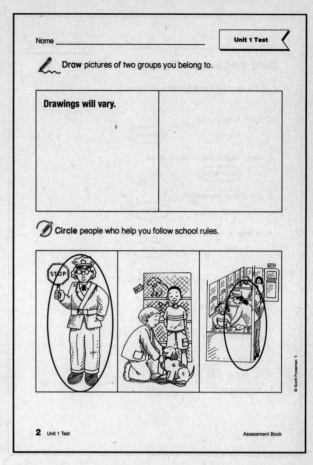

Bottom-left panel

Name _____

Unit 1: Skills Test

Circle a clue that tells what time of day it is.

Write an answer for each question.

FEBRUARY

Sunday	Monday	Tuesday	Wednesday	Thursday	Friday	Saturday
1	2	3	4	5 Constitution Day–Mexico	6	7 Dad's Birthday
8 Susan's party	9	10	11	12	13	14 Valentine's Day
15	16 Presidents' Day	17	18	19	20	21
22	23	24	25	26	27 Tony's class play	28

What is the name of the month? ___**February**___

How many days are in this month? ___**28**___

On what day of the week is Presidents' Day? ___**Monday**___

Bottom-right panel

Name _____

Circle the picture that shows a group.

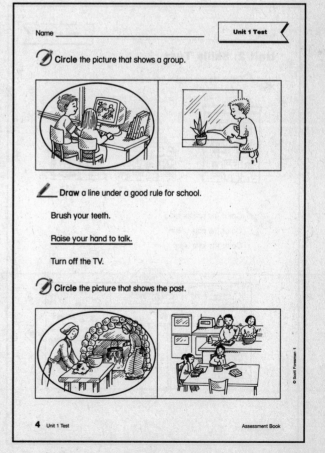

Draw a line under a good rule for school.

Brush your teeth.

<u>Raise your hand to talk.</u>

Turn off the TV.

Circle the picture that shows the past.

Unit 2: Content Test

🖉 **Circle** a word to finish each sentence.

1. North America is a ____.
   law   (continent)

2. Many neighborhoods make up my ____.
   (community)   ocean

3. A mayor is one kind of ____.
   state   (leader)

4. Atlantic is the name of a big ____.
   law   (ocean)

TEST PREP Which word completes each sentence?

1. Littering is against the ____.
   a. leader   (b.) law
   c. ocean   d. state

2. Florida is a ____.
   a. leader   b. lake
   c. continent   (d.) state

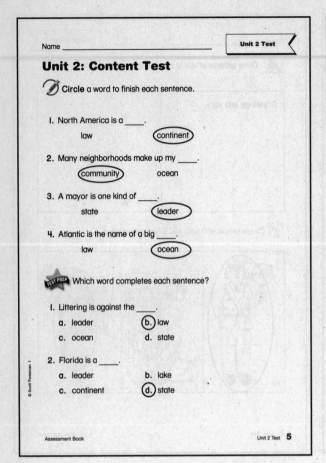

Assessment Book   Unit 2 Test **5**

🖉 **Draw** one person who helps in your neighborhood.
Draw a leader in your community. **Drawings will vary.**

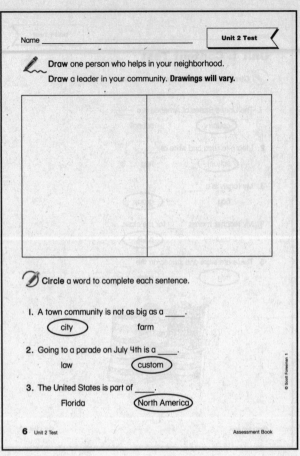

🖉 **Circle** a word to complete each sentence.

1. A town community is not as big as a ____.
   (city)   farm

2. Going to a parade on July 4th is a ____.
   law   (custom)

3. The United States is part of ____.
   Florida   (North America)

6   Unit 2 Test   Assessment Book

Unit 2: Skills Test

🖉 **Color** the two houses that are alike.

🖉 **Color** the school red.
Color the park green.
Color the lake blue.

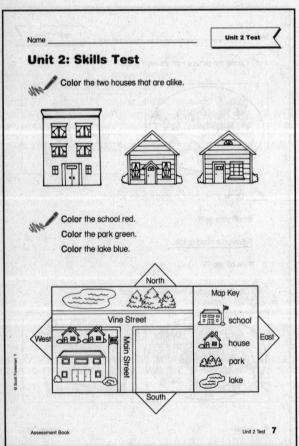

Assessment Book   Unit 2 Test **7**

🔍 **Look** at the map.

🖉 **Write** an answer for each question.

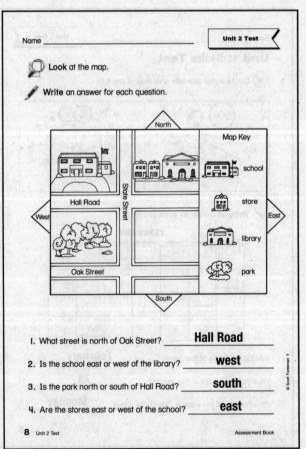

1. What street is north of Oak Street? ____ **Hall Road**

2. Is the school east or west of the library? ____ **west**

3. Is the park north or south of Hall Road? ____ **south**

4. Are the stores east or west of the school? ____ **east**

8   Unit 2 Test   Assessment Book

© Scott Foresman 1

---

26   Answer Key

Assessment Book

Unit 3: Content Test

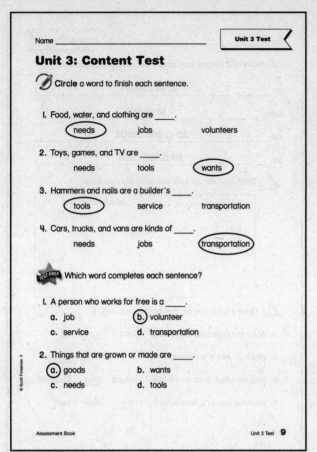

Circle a word to finish each sentence.

1. Food, water, and clothing are ____.
   (needs)   jobs   volunteers

2. Toys, games, and TV are ____.
   needs   tools   (wants)

3. Hammers and nails are a builder's ____.
   (tools)   service   transportation

4. Cars, trucks, and vans are kinds of ____.
   needs   jobs   (transportation)

TEST PREP Which word completes each sentence?

1. A person who works for free is a ____.
   a. job   (b.) volunteer
   c. service   d. transportation

2. Things that are grown or made are ____.
   (a.) goods   b. wants
   c. needs   d. tools

Draw someone making or growing goods.

Draw someone doing a service job. Drawings will vary.

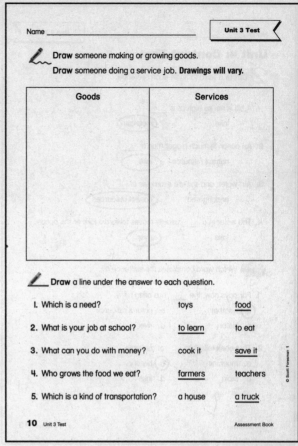

Goods	Services

Draw a line under the answer to each question.

1. Which is a need?   toys   <u>food</u>

2. What is your job at school?   <u>to learn</u>   to eat

3. What can you do with money?   cook it   <u>save it</u>

4. Who grows the food we eat?   <u>farmers</u>   teachers

5. Which is a kind of transportation?   a house   <u>a truck</u>

Unit 3: Skills Test

Write *first*, *next*, and *last* to show the order.

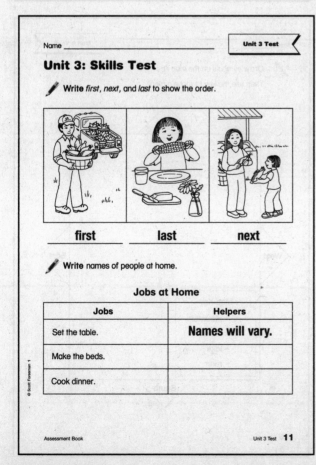

first   **last**   **next**

Write names of people at home.

Jobs at Home

Jobs	Helpers
Set the table.	**Names will vary.**
Make the beds.	
Cook dinner.	

Trace Lee's route on the map.

Write words to complete the sentences.

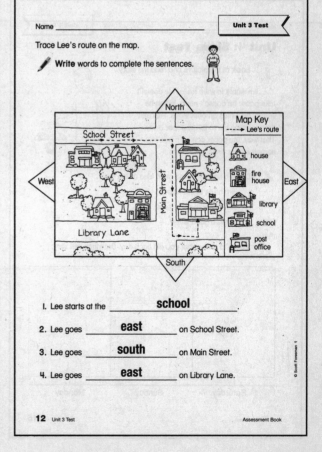

1. Lee starts at the _____ **school** _____

2. Lee goes _____ **east** _____ on School Street.

3. Lee goes _____ **south** _____ on Main Street.

4. Lee goes _____ **east** _____ on Library Lane.

Unit 4: Content Test

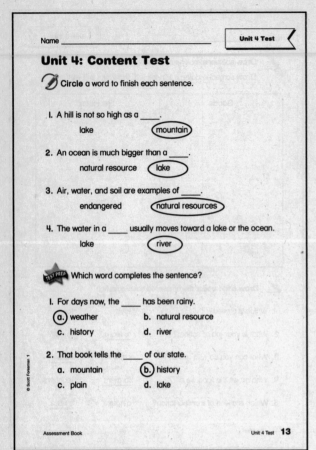

✏ Circle a word to finish each sentence.

1. A hill is not so high as a ____.
   lake   (mountain)

2. An ocean is much bigger than a ____.
   natural resource   (lake)

3. Air, water, and soil are examples of ____.
   endangered   (natural resources)

4. The water in a ____ usually moves toward a lake or the ocean.
   lake   (river)

TEST PREP Which word completes the sentence?

1. For days now, the ____ has been rainy.
   (a.) weather   b. natural resource
   c. history   d. river

2. That book tells the ____ of our state.
   a. mountain   (b.) history
   c. plain   d. lake

Assessment Book   Unit 4 Test **13**

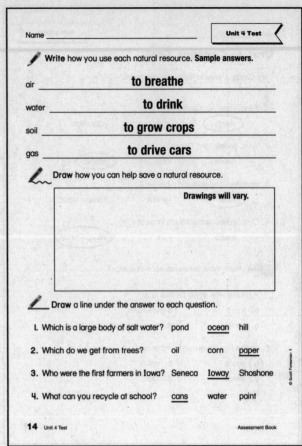

✏ Write how you use each natural resource. **Sample answers.**

air _____ **to breathe** _____

water _____ **to drink** _____

soil _____ **to grow crops** _____

gas _____ **to drive cars** _____

✎ Draw how you can help save a natural resource.

> **Drawings will vary.**

✎ Draw a line under the answer to each question.

1. Which is a large body of salt water?   pond   <u>ocean</u>   hill

2. Which do we get from trees?   oil   corn   <u>paper</u>

3. Who were the first farmers in Iowa?   Seneca   <u>Ioway</u>   Shoshone

4. What can you recycle at school?   <u>cans</u>   water   paint

14 Unit 4 Test   Assessment Book

Unit 4: Skills Test

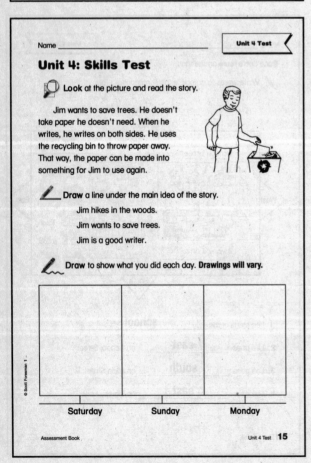

🔍 Look at the picture and read the story.

Jim wants to save trees. He doesn't take paper he doesn't need. When he writes, he writes on both sides. He uses the recycling bin to throw paper away. That way, the paper can be made into something for Jim to use again.

✎ Draw a line under the main idea of the story.

Jim hikes in the woods.

<u>Jim wants to save trees.</u>

Jim is a good writer.

✎ Draw to show what you did each day. **Drawings will vary.**

Saturday	Sunday	Monday

Assessment Book   Unit 4 Test **15**

✎ Draw symbols on the map key.
Then use the key to make a map.

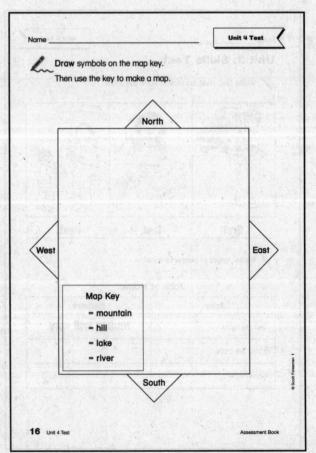

North

West   East

Map Key
= mountain
= hill
= lake
= river

South

16 Unit 4 Test   Assessment Book

---

28 Answer Key

Assessment Book

© Scott Foresman 1

Unit 5: Content Test

Circle a word to finish each sentence.

1. Atlanta is the ____ of the state of Georgia.
   (capital)   colony   vote

2. To vote, a ____ of the United States must be 18 years old.
   holiday   colony   **(citizen)**

3. Presidents' Day is a ____ in February.
   freedom   **(holiday)**   colony

4. A person's right to make choices is called ____.
   (freedom)   capital   holiday

TEST PREP Which word completes the sentence?

1. Virginia was once a ____ of England.
   a. vote   **(b.)** colony
   c. holiday   d. capital

2. George Washington was our first ____.
   a. citizen   b. capital
   c. holiday   **(d.)** President

Write a letter to match each picture with a sentence.

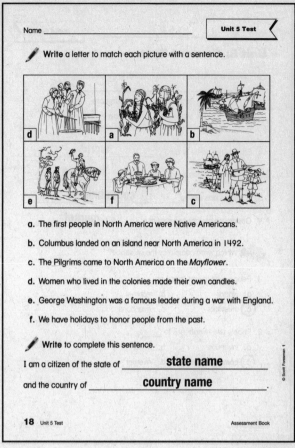

a. The first people in North America were Native Americans.

b. Columbus landed on an island near North America in 1492.

c. The Pilgrims came to North America on the *Mayflower*.

d. Women who lived in the colonies made their own candles.

e. George Washington was a famous leader during a war with England.

f. We have holidays to honor people from the past.

Write to complete this sentence.

I am a citizen of the state of _____**state name**_____

and the country of _____**country name**_____.

Unit 5: Skills Test

Draw three pictures to retell this story.

That first winter was very hard for the Pilgrims. The Wampanoag helped the Pilgrims. They showed Pilgrims what crops to plant. The Pilgrims hunted and fished for other food. Later, they celebrated with the Wampanoag.

1	2	3

Circle the correct words.

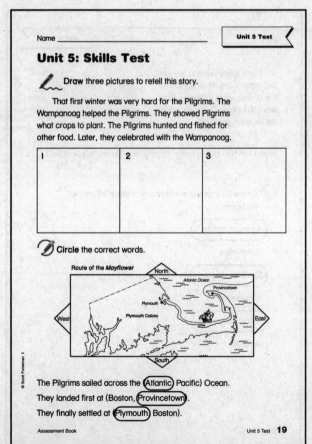

Route of the *Mayflower*

The Pilgrims sailed across the (**Atlantic**) Pacific) Ocean.

They landed first at (Boston, (**Provincetown**)).

They finally settled at ((**Plymouth**) Boston).

Answer the questions about the diagram.

Mayflower

1. What does the diagram show? **parts of the Mayflower**

2. How many masts did the ship have? **3**

3. Why did the ship need sails? **to go; to catch the wind**

4. How long was the *Mayflower*? **90 feet**

Write what you think of this ship.

_____

_____

_____

Unit 6: Content Test

✏️ Write a word from the box to finish each sentence.

market	communicate
world	invention

1. Earth is the name of our _____**world**_____.

2. The printing press was a great _____**invention**_____.

3. Talking is one way to _____**communicate**_____.

4. Goods are bought and sold at a _____**market**_____.

⭐ **TEST PREP** Which word completes the sentence?

1. People who invent things are _____.
   a. worlds   b. markets
   (c.) inventors   d. inventions

2. People use telephones to _____.
   a. invention   b. world
   (c.) communicate d. inventor

🔍 **Look** at each picture and read the question.

✏️ **Circle** the letter of your answer.

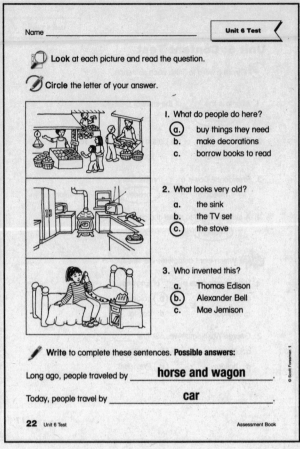

1. What do people do here?
   (a.) buy things they need
   b. make decorations
   c. borrow books to read

2. What looks very old?
   a. the sink
   b. the TV set
   (c.) the stove

3. Who invented this?
   a. Thomas Edison
   (b.) Alexander Bell
   c. Mae Jemison

✏️ Write to complete these sentences. **Possible answers:**

Long ago, people traveled by _____**horse and wagon**_____

Today, people travel by _____**car**_____.

Unit 6: Skills Test

✏️ Write to predict.

Luis has a pen pal. The pen pal lives in Japan. Luis and his pen pal write to each other often. They tell each other about their families and friends.

One day, Luis got a new pet. He was so excited! He drew a picture of his dog. He put himself in the picture too.

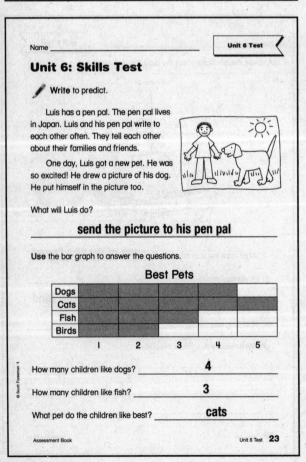

What will Luis do?

_____**send the picture to his pen pal**_____

Use the bar graph to answer the questions.

Best Pets

	1	2	3	4	5
Dogs	■	■	■	■	
Cats	■	■	■	■	■
Fish	■	■	■		
Birds	■	■			

How many children like dogs? _____**4**_____

How many children like fish? _____**3**_____

What pet do the children like best? _____**cats**_____

Nan's family wants to buy a pet. Dad wants a dog. Mom wants a cat. Her brother wants a hamster. Nan wants a goldfish. The family has to decide which pet to buy.

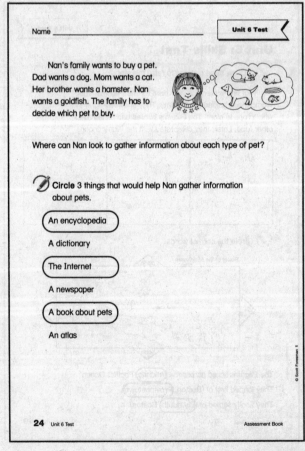

Where can Nan look to gather information about each type of pet?

✏️ Circle 3 things that would help Nan gather information about pets.

(An encyclopedia)

A dictionary

(The Internet)

A newspaper

(A book about pets)

An atlas

NOTES

NOTES

NOTES

NOTES

NOTES

NOTES

NOTES

NOTES

NOTES

NOTES